There's No I in Debris

There's No I in Debris
Except This One!

Poems by
C. SCOTT KINDER-PYLE

Foreword by
CAROL HOWARD MERRITT

Photography by
DAVID S. LORBER

RESOURCE *Publications* • Eugene, Oregon

THERE'S NO I IN DEBRIS
Except This One!

Copyright © 2018 C. Scott Kinder-Pyle. All rights reserved. Except for brief quotations in critical publications or reviews, no part of this book may be reproduced in any manner without prior written permission from the publisher. Write: Permissions, Wipf and Stock Publishers, 199 W. 8th Ave., Suite 3, Eugene, OR 97401.

Resource Publications
An Imprint of Wipf and Stock Publishers
199 W. 8th Ave., Suite 3
Eugene, OR 97401

www.wipfandstock.com

PAPERBACK ISBN: 978-1-5326-6062-7
HARDCOVER ISBN: 978-1-5326-6063-4
EBOOK ISBN: 978-1-5326-6064-1

Manufactured in the U.S.A.   10/16/18

For Sheryl Kinder-Pyle

"...And it speaks in notes struck
or caressed or blown or plucked
off our own bodies: remember
existence already remembers
the flush upon it you will have been,
you who have reached out ahead
and taken up some of the black dust
we become, souvenir
which glitters already in the bones of your
hand."

—Galway Kinnell, "There Are Things I Tell to No One,"
from *Selected Poems*

"The reality of God is always present only in subjective anticipation of the totality of reality, in models of the totality of meaning presupposed in all particular experience. These models however are historic, which means that they are subject to confirmation or refutation by subsequent experience."

—Wolfhart Pannenberg, *Theology and the Philosophy of Science*

"Therefore, every scribe who has been trained in the kingdom of heaven is like the master of a household who brings out of his treasure what is new and what is old."

—Matthew 13:52 (New Revised Standard Version)

"I am a broken vessel, Lord—
Rubble where a soul should be,
This body that I bleed away
For heaven's sake, or sympathy's,
And wreckage never to be found..."

—Jill Alexander Essbaum, "Kenosis," from *Heaven*

Contents

Foreword by Carol Howard Merritt | ix
Acknowledgements | xi

One: Call to Worship
Edict | 2
The Coming In The Clouds Drama, Revised | 4
Eye-Witnesses | 6
The Call for the Other | 8
Three Mysterious Strangers Come Into My Delicatessen | 10
Tomato Ripening on September 11th | 12
Blazing New Trails on the Fire Lane | 14

Two: Prayer of Confession
On the Agenda: the 'Do Not Gather Seaweed' sign | 18
Mischief Night | 20
The Casual Dress of the Dead | 22
Sasquatch, 1967 | 24
The Anti-Freckle Cream Container Found on Nikumaroro | 26
As To Whether Playing Golf Is Recreation: the Verdict | 28
Post-Patriarchal Pictures | 30

Three: Assurance of Pardon
News You Can't Pronounce | 34
Quid Pro Quo | 36
Interview for Job—Paying for Seminary | 38
Homage to the Infinite Mildred Jukes | 40
Hermeneutics | 48
Testimony Transplant | 50
Could've Been A U.S. Senator | 52

Four: Passing the Peace

Time Management Before the Prophecy Seminar | 56

Film Scene of My Father Who Dies Without a Camera in Sight | 58

After Adjunct Teaching, I Say Grace Over Oysters Rockefeller | 60

Jonah, First Person Redux | 62

Exposé | 64

Under a Pseudonym | 66

Among the Lichens | 68

Foreword
Rev. Carol Howard Merritt

Georgia O'Keefe informed us that no one ever sees a flower: "[T]o see takes time, like to have a friend takes time."[1] O'Keefe must draw the petals out of their fields, magnify the colors, and amplify the folds to a size that demands my attention. Then when I stand in stunned awe before the canvas, O'Keefe pries my eyes open to all of the wonder of this tiny thing. The flower—no longer a splotch of confetti color that I barely notice in the corner of my eye as I speed along the highway getting from one job to the next—becomes vibrant and sensual when I see it as a friend.

This is often the artist's mission: to slow us down, waking us to the cruelty, delight, and wonder of our world.

I forget this. I live in a culture of quick consumption that taught me how to commodify everything, especially the minutes that make up a day. I inhabit this odd reality where hours are billable, food is fast, and productivity is measured. I became too busy for the novel, then the blogpost felt too cumbersome. Now the 240-character status update is just long enough for me to consume. I devour newspaper headlines as I run on a treadmill, in order to get a bite-size taste of my world. I never quite savor any of it.

Until the artist reminds me that i I must stop. I have to stand before the canvas for a soul-stirring moment. I must learn to become so immersed that I forget that time is money, and I must delight, savor, and linger.

Painting, music, liturgy, poetry, and photography demands that I stop and look through the lens of another person, noticing the curves until I have a stunning portrait of the world around me that is just close enough so that it is recognizable, but different enough so that it is completely and utterly strange.

---

1. Georgia O'Keefe wrote this for an exhibition catalogue of the show *An American Place* (1944).

Foreword

I felt this deceleration as I read the words of *There is No I in Debris* and studied the photographs. When I got to the end, without hesitation, I began the book again. I wanted to stay lost in this world where damp salt air clung to my skin. I didn't want to leave the protracted hours where I could consider the oyster and the lichen. Through the pages, the subtleties became so enlarged that I remembered eroding coastlines and spaces where teeth once rooted in my mouth. I continued to sit with fresh mysteries of the words on the page and speculating the meanings between each line.

Through his verse, Scott Kinder-Pyle reminds us that poetry is prayer, for it allows us to move into a world of meditation where details become magnified, time loses its measure, and we learn the unhurried delight of making friends with the world surrounding us.

Acknowledgements

I'm extremely grateful to all of my teachers, professors and colleagues who've supported this work. These include Jonathan Johnson and Christopher Howell, from the Inland Center for Writers at Eastern Washington University.

Likewise, the editors of the following literary journals have been courageous (or clumsy) enough to publish versions of these poems: *Cape Rock, Crab Creek Review, Fiddleback, Railtown Almanac. A Spokane Poetry Anthology, Santa Clara Review, Sojourners,* and *Redactions.*

One: Call to Worship

Edict

> The purpose of poetry is to remind us
> how difficult it is to remain just one person,
> for our house is open, there are no keys in the doors,
> and invisible guests come in and out at will.
> —Czeslow Milosz, Ars Poetica

I used to smell the wet maples, the leathery
green primers, saturated with cursive drops
of cloudburst, a lesson in penmanship after every
cleansing rain; and as that sated sensation

hovered one mid afternoon between conscious
thought and oblivion an angel approached
barefoot on the window sill and stood toes
dripping with sap like medicine. He

said, *the only way to meet them all
is to patch the hole through which the
mosquitoes enter and the only way to
block that entrance is to re-write the edict*

*that's been degraded by recent radioactive
leaks in Japan.* He went on, *get your energy
elsewhere, photosynthesis maybe.* I
said, *I'm a mystery to anyone on that coastline, but*

would like to know them if there's time. Then we
broke off communication—I from my end by preaching
a sermon and he from his end by converting
to Dadaism. Now nothing is ever really moist and

every tree's ambivalent about growth in a downpour
although many might interpret leaves as they fall.
King Cyrus issued the last legal declaration yet
there's no use hearing it unless debris cooperates.

The Coming In The Clouds Drama, Revised

So fortunate am I to sit within a glass
atrium and revise dying in my head

while outside the furies of snow swim like
desperate sperm into the ovum tree.
                      Which bodies reproduce here?

I take that back; all but snow is retracted. And
the tree opines for idols of old,

those who might leer and stare long into Yahweh's skies.
The snow now is comprised

of shred letters, torrential outpourings of *Please,* and *Take me back,*
pitiful plaintiffs by which the Lord's unmoved,

and which are pinned down like the dead
specimens of spring thaw.
                      Whose handwriting melts here?

Before it hits the ground, a crystal lingers opposite
the window pane near my face. And though it wasn't
meant for me, I love the word torn between syllables of
script: Tohu va vohu (וְהֹ֖בָנ וּהֹ֔ת). Formless and void.
Welter and waste. This is the drama coming in the clouds.

I take that back; all but clouds is retracted. And
the tree, unable to absorb the break-up,

ties off and shoots up. A vein in the firmament bulges blue.
The false gods promise to always be true despite the fact
that it's over.

And around one arm of this chair I'm wrapped as dinosaurs are pulled

tight with teeth, and as those same go slack when needles from
the tree fall, going from green to brown to white layers of gauze.
                       Why is this all so addictive?

Eye-Witnesses

> *"All at once the veil is torn away, I have understood . . .*
> *I have seen."*
>
> —Jean Paul Sartre

Affinity for someone with a cornea abrasion is like
a divinity degree. It's all a blur

and you regret wanting to go to be healed in the first place
and/or believing the last

will be first
only to be frisked for their credentials.

That's all Jesus down there in the crotch
where the crux of the matter's chaffing in the wind.

What have you got? God has ostensibly spooned out
a deeply set eye-ball and cast it like a bouillon cube
into the world where we see the swirl of vegetable
bits in soup. May I offer you some grandeur, sir?

Some blunder mistaken for thunder from the cloud?
Just add baptismal water and stir. Coming

into focus is a dog's leash, a tether to a tree trunk
being drawn taut and then given slack. Is there

a crumb for the Canaanite crowd? All
the other trees are clapping their hands as if

they had tickets to a sell-out show. You
can still catch it—always about to happen.

The Call for the Other

The call comes to my cell-phone
when I'm driving away.

There's a voice in my head: *Don't answer!*
But a digit depresses: *Is this Michael Lip-pret?*

Press One. . . Traffic's getting tight. Hell No!

If this is not Michael Lip-pret,
Press Two. . .

If you need time to bring Michael Lip-pret
To the phone,
Press Three.

I wait for the option to hang myself.
The automation never gives an inch.

Instead I'm given slack to bring Michael to my cell . . .
I'm offered hours of the day when he might
return the call at his convenience . . .

(How long might I need?)
(Exactly where would I find this guy?)

(If I feign his cadence. . . If I mimic his absence,
might I get off this line?)

(Will there be a fine if I surrender these digits
to the next poor hominid
to come?)

Finally, desperate for self-differentiation, I heave
my device to the side of the road. It careens

off canyon walls—a conflagration,
into the river.

Michael has a lot to answer for.
The cell phone doesn't float.

Three Mysterious Strangers Come Into My Delicatessen

As disheveled seraphim come & go
most every day of the week

these guys on Sunday stood out
for their stogies.

I gave them a wide berth for fear
of second-hand smoke.

They wanted their ham sliced thin
and their mayo thickly smeared.

And so, they appeared to know
Michalangelo.

Will there be anything else?
Something other than hoagies? —

to which one exclaimed for the rest
how there might be more
theophanies to come.

Well, I nearly severed my thumb
while chopping lettuce!

Let us pray! Rogue angels are quite trans-
parent in this respect: they're like elephants
beneath the big top. (Don't think of elephants!)

Most have gone extinct because of treatment
in the three-ring circus. *Who you calling*

extinct? Who you calling

extinct? Who you calling
extinct?

And they were gone when I blinked,
like loose change through a pocket,
without blessing a damn thing.

Tomato Ripening on September 11th

I will de-stem the safe
distance that keeps
this speck of blood
hanging around.

You will catch first-
responder-widows
on T.V. and stew
for hours on end.

I will rinse grime
from the plump baby's
cheek and slice up
seed-speckled pulp.

You will slurp down
that dry German
wine with tablets of
Acetaminophen.

I will toss a salad
with oil and vinegar
dressing into a bowl
gasping for breath.

You will slur combi-
nations of diphthongs
but swear to being
sober and so wrong.

Blazing New Trails on the Fire Lane

Before my fatal heart attack I blaze around the cul-de-sac
and walk upon the trail. The wetlands there are frail
with run-off from each roof. And I wish I were aloof,
like water fowl, to damage. But what's the old adage?
A bird in hand is worth more than a land's reclamation?
Asymmetric ripples scroll eclectic marquees in June.
A woman joins me soon who turns an even fifty.
She's always been thrifty; and Wednesday's no exception
to her predilection: *I hope the farmer never sells . . .*
Does that ring any bells? We bisect cattails and wheat
with barns and tractors' conceit. And we're supposing
this trail's for hosing down our houses in flame.
And so catastrophe's to blame for meadows so paved.
(A hook & ladder might save for no other reason.)
But now's the season to let belongings burn. Out of
compulsion, before we turn, we discern which to spurn.

Two: Prayer of Confession

On the Agenda:
the 'Do Not Gather Seaweed' sign

Mermaids, when they shimmy ashore, lose their eyebrows
on the placard's aluminum shaft.

Visitors'
quizzically-wrinkled

foreheads have been observed at the water's edge:
There is currently a prohibition in six languages

other than our own
which may account for this behavior.

(Mermaids no longer speak the vernacular.)

As scales exfoliate from caudal fins
pristine inner-thighs chafe into chum.

Styrofoam lodges in labia-folds
for the first penetration ever.

Rib-tides pull phosphorescence back to sea, which is beyond our
    jurisdiction.
Eel-grass smears and perforates Port Townsend's boundaries.

Let the Chamber of Commerce take care: the briny protozoa are also
    culpable.

Discussion. Motion to table. Seconded. Approved by Quorum. Plans
to gather in gelatinous dreams of devolution when the moon is blood red.

Meeting adjourned with incantations.

Mischief Night

"I guess that's the thing buried in front of me, half buried in its vast pit. . . .
Someone's crawling out of the hollow top. . . coming. . ."
—From the Mercury Theatre broadcast
of War of the Worlds, Oct. 30, 1938

The war was fabricated on slabs left by idol-factories.
Orson Wells found them in Grovers Mill.

On a distant hill, surrounded by fair-weather
fans, aliens would land—

and he'd make them the most.
Happily they'd romp the emptiness
near the casino dumpsters.

By some happenstance, they'd trim azaleas and plant
metal mailboxes. All was well

for the aliens-who-turned-settlers
just as the prophets had predicted

O land, land, land—

Only a few hooligans hooted
nostalgically for the pre-existent world.

And then, overnight the night changed:

The radio audience grew despondent on air,
    as despots arose on stilts.

Water towers—with their globe-like heads—became menacing
to the mob that forgot disclaimers,

and increasingly
many others bought plasma screens to soothe their fears.

The Casual Dress of the Dead

When they drop their flesh to the floor
like a baggy pair of shorts,

a maroon jersey with the number 88
and a backwards baseball cap. . .

I do my best to hang their scalps on hooks
    in the foyer.

I throw the torso's on the cedar chest
    in the master-bedroom.

But with the limp arms and languid legs
I'm typically at a loss, and can't find any
place where they won't clutter things up
and give off the odor of living through

a humid afternoon. Blood comes out
    in cold water, of course.

But it's not my laundry to do, is it? Why
    can't they do their own?

Finally, in spasms of tidiness, I gather
the strewn muscle-memories in baskets.
It's a pattern with me. I don't even ask.
After all, they're staying in my house.

My house,
    my rules, I say aloud. . .

And yet, the dead-beats only listen
    when it suits them.

Sasquatch, 1967

I've never so much as dipped a toe
in Bluff Creek, California
(let alone a foot

on the Bering Strait).
This is a wild place; no need
for psychedelics—

Roger & Bob rented the relic
and shot 53 seconds to hell.

One flopped on a bed of peat
where whiskey sloshed
against his ribs.

The other spooked horses and sniffed his own
rancid hide. Regardless, I doubt I'm there.
Existence is a stealthy pathogen.

At night porcupines digest bones which mostly belong to me.
Diluvian boulders disappear in dark fecundity.

And so, you're alone because you watch for effect.
Roger & Bob did interviews to that self-fulfilling neglect.
One said I had a look of contempt—like an umpire
with whom players argue a call.

This is a wild place; to enter
you must renounce every game for what you've seen.
Unmake the moment you've come to believe
—perhaps like Roger & Bob—that

I am

a mature female, with breasts that can't be faked—
a gait to lap up the miles, headed west.
Come now: don't plagiarize
the recluse. Breathe,
breathe and be nauseous.

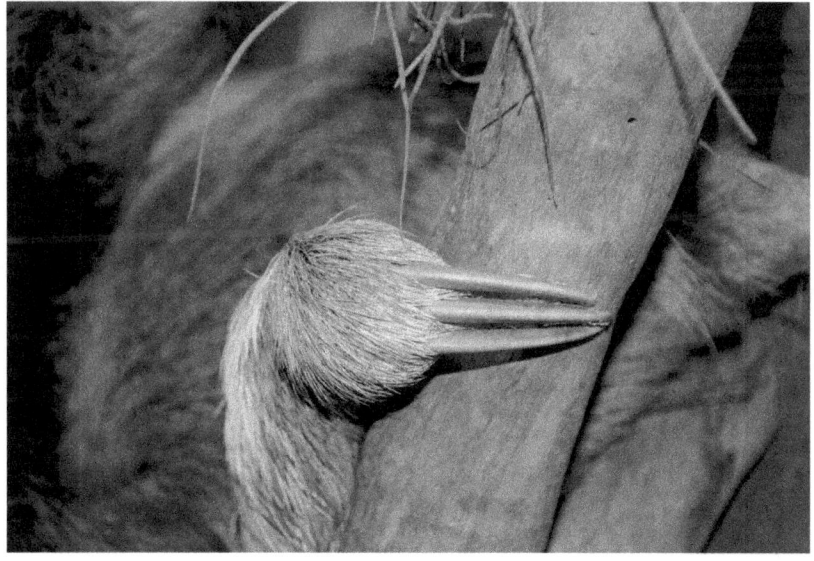

The Anti-Freckle Cream Container Found on Nikumaroro

> "The whole width of the world has passed behind us,
> except this broad ocean..."
> —Amelia Earhart

They could not have picked a better spot
to be stranded with Amelia's skin—
where they became as countless
as the stars above—

She and her navigator (not in love)
but alone—

and picked clean to the bone
by ghostly crabs
together—

Weren't they—long before that
gruesome eventuality—
proving *her* lack of vanity
with a single glass jar?

———

There she is, you see, aglow
with bringing seawater to boil.

———

They found it blackened by old flames
on a coral reef—

the spit of land
where skin-care became luxury—

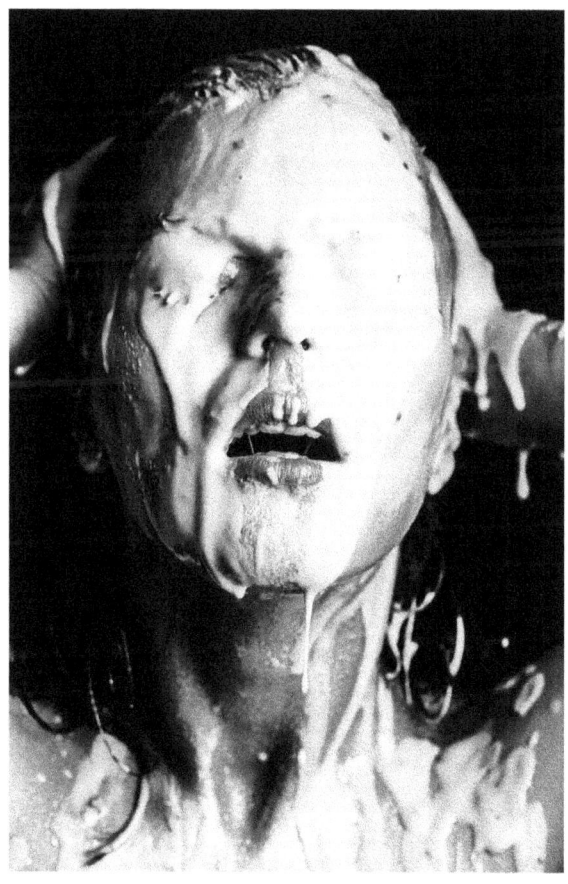

As To Whether Playing Golf Is Recreation: the Verdict

> "Qualchan came to see me at 9 o'clock, at 9:15 he was hung..."
> —Colonel George Wright, 9th Infantry Regiment,
> Washington Territory, Sept. 24, 1858

As to whether
it was under a flag of truce
or not, this is the last sentence
concerning Qualchan:

his actual time of death,
his state of mind before a state could form—

And as to whether, on the adam's-apple-edge,
the knot to choke him with twine
frayed loose in the mist—

and as to his chanting death-songs in defiance—
I don't know. I don't know. I don't know.

But rising from this creek,
a trail of creeping
contingency—the course, ill-defined.

What's the time? A quarter 'til or after?

Certain salt-of-the-earth ahead of me
turf divots in the green. Nine holes

in doubt—the whites of my eyes
await disaster.

Post-Patriarchal Pictures

A mansion might be a bit much for me now
as genes for auto-repair and home
maintenance have skipped
a generation.

Most of the tools remain in packages
and they're admired always
for their potential
usefulness.

Nothing helps: a patriarch offered
a problem-solving formula
in times of need.
He said,

>*I hung that!*

>>referring to a picture of the sea
>>tilted on a wall.

And he said, *That's mine, you get your own!*

>referring to a woman
>who took care of—
>and conquered—him

in the end.
They made love

between two jetties in
Cape May, New Jersey,
and I've been eroding ever
since: Who can fix a coastline?

Can it be straightened like a picture?
All the ocean shades spill over the frame—

gray and gun-metal green.
Blue's too obvious for oblivion.

Three: Assurance of Pardon

News You Can't Pronounce

Reports from *Llullaillaco* are troubling.
Three are dead, but well-preserved.

Lightening struck the girl,
drugs likely rendered

the boy comatose
before he froze.

But in the maiden's stomach, llama
meat and maize.

Her suitors wouldn't leave for days.
Not until they brought her down.

Yet, on the border
between Chile and Argentina
the Incas used to braid her hair.
It snakes to her remnant-hips today.

You can see the cultures taken
with sterile, cotton swabs

on the worldwide web: *mycobacterium*
lives there still, and might *ad infinitum*.

She had a waist the trembling
young ones wrapped their arms
around at 22,000 feet.

It's all wasted now on science.

Quid Pro Quo

Once I smothered my teeth,
one by one, beneath a pillow,

and the pillow's foam took a gun
to my skull and made a cavity.

I awoke a bloody memory-
bank for morsels chewed
or bones gnawed,

my gum-line, tongue and tonsils
complicit for crimes I'd soon commit. Thus,

I confess: *O shit!* I confess: each baby bicuspid was none
the wiser... just gone from my mouth.

And like impulsive words, devoutly spoken,
incisors decamped, and leaving bunkers
in a bombed-out membrane—
molars too...

All this happened without me
playing a conscious role.

There were no fisticuffs, no braggadocios brawls,
and not a single bit of elbow grease
expertly applied.

Of course, a well-meaning hygienist once tried
her technique. At his peak a suicidal dentist swiveled
the hydraulic chair. But mostly I sucked the cold night-air
after visits,

and knew something irregular

had occurred.

    Believe me when I say, it was *not* the water's
fluoridation—had nothing to do with method
of sedation.

    It was *quid pro quo*. All for show. Once
I bargained for a coin to appear

       —my ferry-ride over—

    but received instead my venial veneer.

Interview for Job—Paying for Seminary

It's not a job for Oedipus Rex

      just off Princeton Junction
          where clergy learn to function:

security for the office complex.

      So, do you have any scruples
          about, you know, the missiles?

Not if I can read the epistles.

They're more or less steeples
anyway,

      and the *Way*'s whatever
          truth grows like a weed one-
      hundred-fold, until it's fun!

      Are you good working Sunday
          mornings, when Jesus is risen?

Well, that's a matter of division

in church circles, but let me say
I can be in Galilee the day after

      Next—

Homage to the Infinite Mildred Jukes

1.

Mildred Jukes had leverage
No middle-aged woman should
In kindergarten classes. The kids sat cross-legged

Before her concealed curves—a mix of
Velour perhaps without end—and she taught them
To undulate *Amen* with their girl & boy bodies.

But when passages happened on the allegedly
Safe—that blessed bastion known as *the
Bosom of Abraham*

Jesus mentions, they'd groan a little
Looking up into the dark vertical
line of her cleavage,

and they'd wonder: are we all so gendered
and so weaned of nurture if even this bearded
man suckled the oozing sores?

Thereafter—as if by power of suggestion—
a few managed to ooze with sores themselves.

And a few more would enter the chasm as if
going to college. They had carnal knowledge

by which they tried to fix the breach
and perhaps catapult themselves home
from the inside, but

Missus Jukes had a hemorrhage.

2.

I summon you now, Mildred

To a showdown! Or a meltdown!
Whatever comes of the plunder
You taught us to take?

One by one our fingernails curl
Like question marks on the floor.

There are dogs and flames to lick us
Even if someone rises from the dead.

3.

Dearest Mrs. Jukes:
It's been a half a millennium
And still no word from you.

Are you leather-faced and
Mummified in some hyperbaric
Chamber? Should we

Study the absence
Of your reply any further?

Your womb,
We trust, remains barren
Like the day you were born;
And your vagina, all sweet-
Honeysuckle perfume. Many

Other intimate things come
To mind as well, and though
They seem imprudent to ask

We ask anyway
With nothing better to do

On behalf of old cross-legged
Classmates the world-over
While (as yet) we have breath.
Until death, Mrs. Jukes

Until death, and then some—

Faithfully Yours

4.

Damn it, Mildred!

Why no response
From your flesh?

Are you finally now
All Spirit

And too ashamed
To admit you

Grew black hair
On your chest?

Listen! I believe!
I have ears to hear!

You can come out
Now in full view!

Damn it, Mildred!

To thank you
For being nothing

But a pair
Of voluptuous

Turtledoves is not
My intention.

Hermeneutics

"There is only one woman in the world. One woman, with many faces."
—Nikos Kazantzakis, *The Last Temptation of Christ*

"Recognize what is in your sight, and that which is hidden from you will become plain..."
—Anonymous, *Nag Hammadi Codice Library*

Before I learned the gist
of various codices

we drove on impish desire
down the road to *Wesley's*.

We tried to kiss but gnashed teeth instead
—and then the exit ramp to Belize

filled the windshield of our faces...

This other woman (not the same
as the one above) burnt the Nag Hammadi
Scrolls her son brought in. They were Bedouins
in British Palestine, who enjoyed their tea.

Now, get a whiff of that manure
on Route 1, going south.

It sure clears out the nostrils on a humid night
when the car makes its own wind—

and ancient—primordial—will be the woman
who demurs when I interpret her signs
of augury.

I remain a goat, and I have no guts left.

Testimony Transplant

> "You only lose what you cling to."
> —Siddhartha Gautama

Let's cut away to Buddha's vision
in which

I go to see Doreen at the hospital.
She's been awaiting a liver
transplant,

and waiting... and while waiting
in Intensive Care, one arrives.

It comes from a little boy
who once played in traffic
or died there,

and the parents donated his organs.
Doreen didn't comprehend
this sending at the time.

Just her husband's kiss
on the cheek. And then I prayed

to Jesus, *Dear Jesus, thank you
for your healing touch...*

It wasn't much, interjected the Buddha
with a jade smile. *I was in the neighborhood.*

And later, Doreen said she felt
vapor-drunk and wise

in her vast womb. And
a boy grew like a bud-tendril
beneath

her tapered shut eyes. They named him Jake.
And he's a liver, and the Lord's to take.

Could've Been A U.S. Senator

The church had a janitor,
who save his parenting
by a college registrar,
could've been a U.S. senator.

He had a mustache to fillet the holy
communion crumb.

It was festooned with spittle-
stalactites from his last mint-julep

on the wrap-around porch. That day
he took vows before a justice of the peace
uneven sidewalks rose to meet his wagon
of supplies—and there were spies!

Who came to send her away
in the form of his senile mother?

She resembled the swan
from the campus pond—

the one with pinioned wings
is her today! Or is it
any hour-glass figure in the night
who will pay her dues if you squint

against the bare light-bulb's glow?
The pulpit had a revolving door

of ministers, but only one righteous
enough to dust & polish pews...

Many came to see his handiwork,

a bulwark never failing to forget:
he could've been a U.S. senator.
He *became* the church's janitor.

Four: Passing the Peace

Time Management Before the Prophecy Seminar

> "And then, perhaps because his breath began
> To fail him, he stopped and hunched against a bush
> As if to make himself and its branches one"
> —The Inferno of Dante, Canto XIII

The bur is borne as flag pins often are
through glass double-doors.

It clings to Virgil's woolen pant-leg
as it does to mine.

(You bristle, of course, not at the sight,
but at my calling your attention to it with words.)

Why dress up for the prophecy seminar?

The hedgerow has starlings enough for
every soft-mouthed bitch in the flatbed.

We ain't got time to go home and change.

And when this tribulation-speech is done
we'll each traipse the field beyond
the church parking lot.

Then, if Jesus arrives in clouds of glory,
Virgil might have a fun story to tell—

And Beatrice, I believe, loves a gamey bird
Shhh! Listen up! Not a word!

Film Scene of My Father Who Dies Without a Camera in Sight

Away from the room without walls
into exile

the machines around him chirp
for intravenous tubes
and take flight.

Their wings are wheels within wheels
on linoleum floors.

We are an aperture—the *P.O.V.* of a worm
in whichever psalm refers to *worm*.

From its mildewed semiotics we then pan
up to giant pores; ruddy scars
appear like a martian
landscape.

Another planet eclipses him (the dying body):
we know this person as *me*, a minuscule piece
of baby-booming debris.

In previous scenes *he* has sugar-dusted
the world with replacements
for rocks and grass. Today

he desires surgery to become
a Palestinian Jew.   *Cut to:*

A mop & bucket, sloshing water.
(Intimations of *Behemoth* and *Leviathan*
lurk beneath the surface.

Fade to black:

The movie-going peers peel off toward their parking spots.
A Palestinian Jew is among the throng who exit.
They are all writhing morsels of worship.

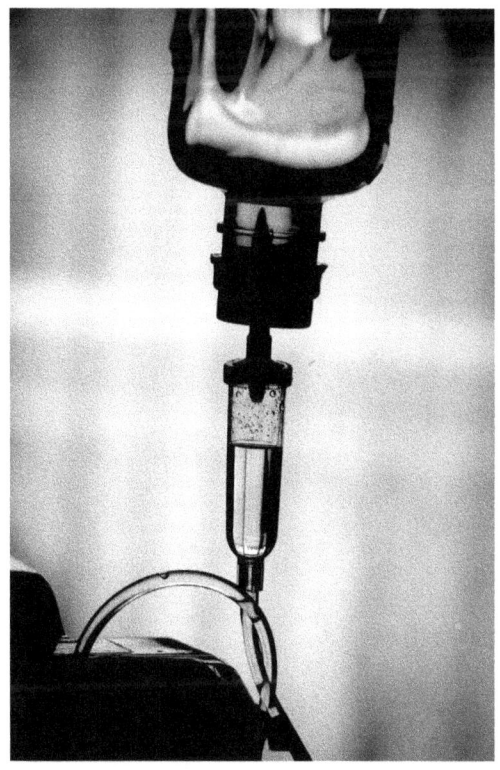

After Adjunct Teaching, I Say Grace Over Oysters Rockefeller

> "Why, then, the world's mine oyster,
> Which I with sword will open."
> —The Wives of Windsor. Act II. Scene II, William Shakespeare

The shellfish today comes gratis.
But maybe brackish beds will rent
to pluvial meat...

        a lattice-
work to help amorphous ascent?

Every face at lecture's interspersed
with sundry grains of sand.

Elicit funds disburse
for erudition done well.

        Remand
to shucking the usual fatigue
and most likely I'll binge
on dirt. Acquit this colloquy
of bivalves, and much will hinge

upon the nacre's vagrant whirl
—even the iconoclastic pearl—

Jonah, First Person Redux

I tried to convert the shark
but it ate me anyway
and every way under the sun
after saying grace.

And then each row of razor sharp teeth —
the esophageal conduit
into the gullet going
down,

but to no avail. I'm now available in Idaho
for weddings and worship services.

Conversion's now a shellfish of my hero-self
who swims the Australian Crawl as good
as William Stafford stays afloat.

No one should be a gateway
drug to being conscious: the plankton
with potential to save the ocean
from plastic has neither hope nor
despair in its bottles.

I do have a message though
and I'll tell it all slant

as light through shudders—

    through the shudders of the deep.
    We do not weep for the end

but for the echoic, indecipherable songs
and for the furthest limits of the sea
which have been conquered

by these miracles of evolution
and by their circling

back with dorsal fins
on the event-horizon.

Exposé

> "Soft-spoken, not the type to cause a scene..."
> —Stanley Kunitz, *To The Reader*

When I get up these days
The concealment scratches at the lid
Of my bulbous skull, and then
From inside my breastbone
A knowing sort of knock
Awaits a word from my adoring
Consciousness: *Just a minute...*

But I never do open up that space
Where noumena haunt like jackals
Just inside the crevasse, my body.

Whatever is asking for revelation
Endures in darkness that's not dark
To itself, and perhaps conjures
A dimly lit nineteenth-century
Parlor for its environs. I go back
To bed when the candles burn
Out around a wooden casket.

There will be a wake with booze,
Broken bottles on the floor, and
Someday perhaps, folks will travel

To see the hidden corpse clipping
Its fungal-toe-nails for the umpteenth
Time, and they'll know, and write
Obituaries to the effect that I was
Never & always a drain to them—
Akin to a propane tank left on

The patio in the recent rain.

Was the concealment instrumental
To my legacy, which amounts to
Being an object in their worlds?

Hell if I know what counts
As phenomena anymore!
But the fact is—you yourself, dear
Reader (to this point), are concealing
A dungeon of wizened demons
And they're all commiserating
With your internal organs, plotting
A story that is your undoing.

Under a Pseudonym

"Life can be understood backwards, but it must be lived forwards. . ."
—Soren Kierkegaard

By then, when there is no *before* and *after*,
he'll have the system down—

>down to a door obliterated by a hurricane—
>down to a hinge and some trim—
>down to the barest pseudonym—

But still wreaking of Copenhagen, I'll get up
the gumption to ask who's fiancé are you
really—

Regine Olsen's or *Mount Moriah*'s?

And, God forbid, if he claims *Both*.

>*Both* would be blasphemy.
>*Both* would be melancholy.
>*Both* would be shekinah glory.

>And supposedly, we're beyond all that now.
>Supposedly, we're immersed again in waters—

and can swim
under a pseudonym.

Among the Lichens

I love the ruins in Scotland
where it's mandatory

I become illusory

among the lichens
on the Abby walls.

There's always room for one more
proleptic filament—

Here I am, Lord!
Woe is—
Send me—

www.ingramcontent.com/pod-product-compliance
Lightning Source LLC
Chambersburg PA
CBHW051703090426
42736CB00013B/2516